The Vegan Airfryer Cookbook

Healthy Recipes From Your Air Frying Lid

MAGGIE PIPER

Copyright © 2019 Maggie Piper

All rights reserved. No part of this publication may be reproduced, distributed, or transmitted in any form or by any means, including photocopying, recording, or other electronic or mechanical methods, without the prior written permission of the publisher, except in the case of brief quotations embodied in critical reviews and certain other noncommercial uses permitted by copyright law.

Limit of Liability/Disclaimer of Warranty: While the publisher and author have used their best efforts in preparing this book, they make no representations or warranties with respect to the accuracy or completeness of the contents of this book and specifically disclaim any implied warranties of merchantability or fitness for a particular purpose. No warranty may be created or extended by sales representatives or written sales materials. The advice and strategies contained herein may not be suitable for your situation. You should consult with a professional where appropriate. Neither the publisher nor author shall be liable for any loss of profit or any other commercial damages, including but not limited to special, incidental, consequential, or other damages

ISBN: 9798629793625

DEDICATION

Thank you Lord, you've always been there!

TABLE OF CONTENTS

INTRODUCTION 1

BREAKFAST/ BRUNCH 5

    Toasted Coconut French Toast 6

    Cauliflower Hash Browns 7

    Fatteh Hummus 8

    Vegan Bacon 9

    English Sandwich Breakfast 11

    Semolina Indian Cutlets 13

    Smoky Tempeh Sandwich 14

    Breakfast Hash Brown 16

    Breakfast Potatoes 18

    Indian Bread/Potato Rolls 19

    Vegan Casserole With Quinoa 21

ENTREES 23

    Creamy Fried Lasagna 24

    Lasagna With Pasta Sauce 26

    Chewy Panko Tofu 28

    Cauliflower Steaks With Mushroom Cashew Gravy 30

    Roasted Veggies Pasta Salad 32

    Quick & Easy Crispy Tofu 34

    Rebaked Stuffed Potatoes 35

    Cauliflower Buffalo Wings With Cashew Cream Sauce 37

    Mashed Potato Dinner 39

- Oil-Free Tofu In Lemon Sauce 41
- Baked Potato With Toppings 43
- Vegetable Kebab 45
- Flavored Cauliflower Stir-Fry 46
- Orange Tofu 47
- Stuffed Eggplant 49

SIDES 51
- Vegan Cauliflower Gnocchi 52
- Sweet Potato Curry Fries With Cumin Dip 53
- Crunchy Fish Taco Wrap With Mango Salsa 55
- Vermouth & Garlic Flavored Mushroom 57
- Fried Vegan Ravioli 58
- Roasted Asparagus 59
- Spicy Bok Choy 60
- Green Bean And Mushroom Bowl 61
- Garlic Thyme Tomatoes 62
- Sweet & Spicy Roasted Acorn Squash 63
- Cauliflower Wings 64
- Crispy Sweet Plantains 65
- Lemon Green Beans 66

APPETIZERS 67
- Crispy Fried Beer Pickles 68
- Crispy Green Tomatoes 69
- Roasted Broccoli 70
- Crispy Pickles 72
- Grilled Corn 73

Air Crisp Falafel	74
Onion Rings	76
Crunchy Buffalo Cauliflower	77
Cubed Butternut Squash	78
Low Carb Vegetable Kebabs	79
Roasted Carrots with Thyme & Parsley	80
Crispy Fried Okra	81
Whiskey Garlic Tofu	82
SNACKS	85
Keto Shishito Peppers	86
Roasted Almonds	87
Crunchy Croutons	88
Bow Tie Pasta Chips	89
Indian Beetroot Chips	90
Air Fried Baby Carrots	91
Toasty Pecan	92
Roasted Chickpeas	93
Chili Lime Roasted Cashew	94
Easy Crunchy Kale Chips	95
Kale/ Potato Nuggets	96
Cinnamon Roasted Apples	98
Savory Rosemary Cashews	99
Vegan Cashew Bacon	100
Crunchy Sweet Potato Fries	101
Crispy Salty Potato Peels	102
Fried Green Tomatoes With Panko Coating	103

DESSERTS 105

    Vanilla Bean Cake 106

    Blackberry Apricot Crumble 107

    Vegan Carrot Cake 108

    Glazed Donuts 109

    Pineapple Sticks With Yoghurt Dip 110

    Coconut Pineapples & Yoghurt Dip 111

    Apple/ Berries Crumble 112

    Moist Coffee Choco Cake 113

    Fried Doughnuts 114

    Crunchy Cookies 115

    Spiced Apples 116

    Marshmallow Chocolate Bread Pudding 117

    Crispy Caramelized Bananas 118

    Banana S'mores 119

    Pumpkin Spice Baked Apples 120

    Chocolate Mug Cake 121

INTRODUCTION

Air-frying is a healthier, low calorie alternative to deep frying. Deep frying uses up huge amounts of oils, which have been proven to be unhealthy. Deep frying is messy and requires plenty of clean-up. The house also comes with a certain smell that tends to linger for a few days, even when it is ventilated. However, air- frying produces crispy foods with very little oil. The texture of air fried foods are generally light and crisp. An increasing number of people are becoming more aware of these differences and facts, and that is why air fryers are becoming more popular in homes.

Technically, air-fryers do not fry. Frying requires cooking foods in fats and air fryers do not really need oil or fats for cooking. So it really isn't frying in all sense of the word. Air fryers are simply countertop convection ovens with a fan to circulate very hot air to cook the food in the fryer basket, quickly, from the outside in. The results are healthy, crispy foods, without the mess.

Air fryers come in different brands, shapes and sizes. There are several kinds in the market. However, one brand stands out from others; in terms of uniqueness, portability and cost. This is the removable Crisp Lid. The Lid is exceptional! It works with the multipot, or any 6 or 8 quart pressure cooker, with a stainless steel inner pot. It is an add-on air fryer that you place on top of the inner pot of your pressure cooker or multipot.

This Removable lid addresses your crisping, broiling and air-frying needs and delivers perfectly cooked foods all the time. It offers several advantages. Since it is an air fryer, it cooks with little or no oil, providing you with low-fat versions of your best foods. It can fry, roast, bake or grill ingredients, providing you with several cooking functions. It is affordable.

It can be cleaned easily. It requires less storage space, since it is just a lid--but not just.

It is a simple equipment, but unique in design and usage. It consists of the main housing with control panel, heating element and a fan that's attached to a glass lid. The heating element performs the air frying function. The fan circulates the heat. Other necessary tools, such as the handle, makes it possible to place the Lid directly on top of the stainless steel inner pot. The control panel, on its own part, has 6 buttons (temperature, time, +/-, stop, and start) and an LED screen to display the most recent time or temperature.

Once you buy one, you also get a 3-inch raised trivet, a silicon trivet, a fryer basket, stainless steel tongs and also a recipe booklet. The trivet is placed in the stainless steel inner pot. The fryer basket is placed on the trivet and this is what holds the food. The stainless steel tongs is for flipping and turning the food in the basket. Flipping is essential in air frying; and cooking with the Removable Crisp Lid requires flipping the foods every now and then. The silicon trivet or mat is used to place the hot Lid when it lifted and removed from the pot. Do not place it anywhere else as the hot Lid can burn any other kitchen surface or equipment. The silicon trivet holds it till it cools. This is particularly important, when you need to flip or shake the food being cooked.

By far, the most unique feature of this device is its transparent lid. While other air fryers do not have a means to see and check the progress of the food being cooked. The manufacturers have addressed this need. The glass lid enables you to see the food and check its progress. Whether you are crisping, broiling or baking foods, you can monitor it all through the glass lid. However, it should not be touched as it gets very hot. Another feature that stands it out from others is that the heat temperature extends to 500°F. It begins from 300 to 500°F, and can be adjusted in in 25 degree increments. But if cooking food with temperature above 450°F, it can only cook for 20 minutes at a stretch, and will turn off afterwards. This is for safety reasons. If you would be cooking for longer time, simply wait for 10 minutes and then turn it on again.

To use, place the inner pot in, place the trivet in the pot, place the mesh fryer basket or pan on the trivet and then place the Crisp Lid on the pot and plug it. Use the controls to set the temperature and adjust cook time (from 1 - 60 minutes). Press the triangle start button to begin As soon as this is done, the heat will be distributed throughout the pot to cook tender and nourishing meals.

Consuming mostly plant foods every day is crucial to good health. With the Removable Lid, it is now easier to cook healthy plant-based air-fried foods that suits your vegan lifestyle. Whether you enjoy French fries, chips or breaded veggies, have the pleasure of also saving money and space by using a Crisp Lid.

Below are a rich collection of air fried vegan recipes. There are quick-and-easy breakfasts, main meals, side dishes, appetizers, snacks and desserts. Use the recipes in this cookbook to add to the ones you are given upon purchase. This cookbook contain some new dishes that will add to your culinary adventure. They come with new and exciting blend or flavors that will please your palate. The Removable Lid makes air frying so much easier and you definitely will love it.

Have fun and stay healthy!

Maggie Piper

BREAKFAST/ BRUNCH

Toasted Coconut French Toast

The healthiest and crispiest 4-ingredient French toast ever!

Prep Time: 4 minutes

Cook Time: 5 minutes

Servings: 1

Ingredients

2 slices gluten-free bread

1/2 cup of lite culinary coconut milk

1 teaspoon of baking powder

1/2 cup shredded coconut, unsweetened

Preparation

1. Combine the baking powder and coconut milk together in a bowl.

2. Place the shredded coconut on a plate, spread out nicely.

3. Take a bread slice and soak in the coconut milk mix and then place on the coconut plate to coat. Place in the fryer basket.

4. Place the pressure cooker trivet in the inner steel pot. Place the basket on the trivet. Place the Crisp Lid on top of the inner pot and plug it in. Set to 350°F and cook for 4 minutes.

5. Remove and enjoy, topped with maple syrup.

Per Serving: Calories 400; Total Fat; 24g Protein 7g; Total Carb 46g; Sodium: 783 mg; Cholesterol: 20mg; Fiber: 9g

Cauliflower Hash Browns

Enjoy a flavorful breakfast of healthy cauliflower hash browns. They are crisp on the outside, yet moist inside.

Prep Time: 10 minutes

Cook Time: 25 minutes

Servings: 8

Ingredients

1/2 head cauliflower

1/2 medium onion, chopped

1/4 cup of chickpea flour

1 tablespoon arrowroot starch

1 tablespoon nutritional yeast flakes

1/2 teaspoon garlic powder

1 teaspoon ground paprika

Salt to taste

Preparation

1. Break cauliflower, place in a colander and rinse under running water. Drain, and pat to remove excess water.

2. Pulse in a food processor, together with the onion and process. This should yield 3 to 4 cups cauliflower rice.

3. Transfer to a bowl, add the rest of the ingredients and mix until it holds together. Divide into portions and shape into flat rectangular shapes of 1/2 inch thickness. Spray fryer basket with cooking spray.

4. Place in the fryer basket and place on the trivet (you may need to work in batches). Plug in Crisp Lid and cook at 375°F for 25 minutes, flipping halfway

Per Serving: Calories 39; Total Fat; Protein 2g; Total Carb 7g; Sodium: mg Fiber: g

Fatteh Hummus

A tasty and nourishing breakfast pudding that can be enjoyed with bread.

Prep Time: 10 minutes

Cook Time: 15 minutes

Servings: 4

Ingredients

2 cups of diced Turkish whole meal bread

Cooking spray

Hummus:

2 cups of whisked coconut yogurt

2 cups of chickpeas, canned or boiled drained

½ - ¾ cup of water, optional

2 garlic cloves

2 tablespoons of lime juice

1 teaspoon of cumin seeds, roasted lightly and crushed

1 teaspoon of chili flakes, optional

Salt

Preparation

1. Bake the bread with your Crisp Lid air fryer at 395°F for 15 minutes.

2. Add the yogurt, chickpeas, lime juice, garlic and salt to a blender and blend until smooth. Add water if necessary.

3. Now place the baked bread at the bottom of a flat dish and then pour the blended yogurt mix over it. Next, place another layer of the baked bread over this mix and then drizzle the remaining yogurt mixture over it.

4. Finally, sprinkle the cumin seeds on it. Drizzle the olive oil and top with the chili flakes and sea salt.

Per Serving: Calories 510; Total Fat; 12g; Protein 26g; Total Carb 77g; Sodium: 104mg; Cholesterol: 5mg; Fiber: 18g

Vegan Bacon
Enjoy bacon with tempeh; that's the vegan way!

Prep Time: 25 minutes

Cook Time: 10 minutes

Servings: 4

Ingredients

1/2 cup of vegetable oil

1 tablespoon of vegan Worcestershire sauce

1/2 cup maple syrup

1 tablespoon of liquid smoke

1/2 tablespoon of cayenne pepper

16 oz. Tempeh

Preparation

1. Combine the oil, Worcestershire sauce, maple syrup, liquid smoke and the cayenne pepper in a shallow bowl.

2. Cut the tempeh thickly into slices of 1/4 inches and place in the bowl of liquids. Let it marinate for 10-15 minutes

3. Remove and place in batches in the fryer basket. Place the pressure cooker trivet in the inner steel pot. Place the basket on the trivet. Place the Crisp Lid on top of the inner pot and plug it in.

4. Cook at 320°F for 10 minutes, flipping halfway through cooking.

Per Serving: Calories 579; Total Fat 40g; Protein 21g; Total Carb 39g; Sodium: 64mg:

Vegan Bacon

English Sandwich Breakfast

A vegan breakfast sandwich of air-fried marinated tofu, which takes the place of the egg, and sliced avocado spread on an English muffin.

Prep Time: 30 minutes

Cook Time: 10 minutes

Servings: 2

Ingredients

Tofu:

½ block extra firm tofu, pressed & sliced into 4, then cut into rounds

½ teaspoon garlic powder

1/8 cup of light soy sauce

1/4 teaspoon turmeric

Dash of paprika

Breakfast Sandwich:

2 vegan English muffins

Vegan mayonnaise, optional

2 vegan cheese slices

1 Haas avocado, sliced

Sliced tomato, optional

Sliced onion, optional

Preparation

1. In a shallow dish, combine the tofu rounds, together with the garlic powder, soy sauce, paprika and turmeric. Marinate, covered for 10 minutes.

2. Place the tofu in the fryer basket. Place the pressure cooker trivet in the inner steel pot. Place the basket on the trivet. Place the Crisp Lid on top of the inner pot and plug it in.

3. Set to 400°F and cook for 10 minutes, shaking halfway.

4. Spread the English muffins with the vegan mayo. Add the avocado, vegan cheese, and desired toppings. Add the cooked tofu as well.

5. Enjoy! Use the leftover marinated tofu to make a tofu scramble.

Per Serving: Calories 423; Total Fat; 18g; Protein 18g; Total Carb 46g; Sodium: 916mg; Cholesterol: 5mg; Fiber: 5g

Semolina Indian Cutlets
A weekend breakfast to relish!

Prep Time: 15 minutes

Cook Time: 23 minutes

Servings: 2

Ingredients:

1 cup of semolina

5 cups of soy milk

½ cup of refined oil

½ cup of mixed vegetables, chopped

½ teaspoon of salt

½ teaspoon of black pepper

Preparation

1. Place your pressure cooker on sauté, add the milk and let it heat through. Add the vegetables and cook for 3 minutes or until all the vegetables are tender. Add the salt and pepper.

2. Pour in the semolina, let it cook until thickened. Turn off sauté, unplug pressure cooker and remove and spread content on a greased plate. Place in the refrigerator for 3-4 hours to harden; or freeze quickly in the freezer.

3. Once firm, remove and cut into your preferred cutlet shape. Coat the cutlets with oil and transfer to the fryer basket.

4. Place the pressure cooker trivet in the inner steel pot. Place the basket on the trivet. Place the Crisp Lid on top of the inner pot and plug it in.

5. Cook at 356°F for 15 minutes.

Per Serving: Calories 1120; Total Fat; 67g; Protein 39g; Total Carb 96g; Sodium: 928mg; Cholesterol: 0mg; Fiber: 12g

Smoky Tempeh Sandwich

Tempeh has a naturally bitter taste, so it must be cooked right for it to be tasty. This is why it should be well-marinated to make it delightful. Enjoy the smoky goodness of this recipe.

Prep Time: 40 minutes

Cook Time: 15 minutes

Servings: 2

Ingredients

1 tablespoon rice vinegar

2 tablespoons soy sauce

1 tablespoon ketchup

1/2 teaspoon paprika

1/2 teaspoon garlic powder

1/2 teaspoon liquid smoke

8 oz. block of tempeh

4 slices whole grain bread

4 lettuce leaves

4 tomato slices

1 avocado

Condiments (such as mayo, mustard, salt & pepper)

Preparation

1. In a large bowl, add together the rice vinegar, soy sauce, paprika, garlic powder, ketchup and liquid smoke.

2. Slice the tempeh thinly and place in the marinade to sit for an hour.

3. Place tempeh strips in the fryer basket. Place the pressure cooker trivet in the inner steel pot. Place the basket on the trivet. Place the Crisp Lid on top of the inner pot and plug it in.

4. Set to 350°F and cook for 10- 12 minutes. Check every 3 minutes to ensure it does not burn.

5. Remove, toast the bread slices, if desired.

6. Slice the avocado and assemble each of the sandwich with ½ of the avocado. Now, place the tomatoes, lettuce and tempeh slices on top. Add desired condiments, top with bread slice.

7. *Enjoy!*

Per Serving: Calories 469; Total Fat; 15g; Protein 21g; Total Carb 70g; Sodium: 1489mg; Cholesterol: 0mg; Fiber: 19g

Breakfast Hash Brown

Delight your kids with these healthy breakfast hash browns.

Prep Time: 35 minutes

Cook Time: 25 minutes

Servings: 4 pieces

Ingredients

2 large potatoes, peeled & shredded

1 tablespoon of flour

Salt & pepper powder, to taste

1 teaspoon of chili flakes

½ teaspoon of garlic powder

½ teaspoon of onion powder

Cooking spray

Preparation

1. Soak the potatoes in cold water and drain. Repeat.

2. Set your pressure cooker on sauté. Add a little oil, add the potatoes and cook for about 5 minutes.

3. Remove potatoes to a plate to cool. Unplug pressure cooker.

4. Combine the corn flour, garlic, onion powder, chili flakes, salt and pepper in a bowl and mix thoroughly.

5. Spread over the plate of potatoes and refrigerate for 25 minutes.

6. Divide the refrigerated potato into equal pieces. Use a knife for this.

7. Place the hash brown in the fryer basket, Spray with cooking oil. Place the pressure cooker trivet in the inner steel pot. Place the basket on the trivet. Place the Crisp Lid on top of the inner pot and plug it in.

8. Cook at 375°F for 20 minutes, flipping halfway through. Serve with ketchup.

Per Serving: Calories 63; Total Fat; 0g; Protein 2g; Total Carb 15g; Sodium: 878mg; Cholesterol: 0mg; Fiber: 1g

Breakfast Potatoes

Breakfast Potatoes

Great-tasting sunrise potatoes!

Prep Time: 5 minutes

Cook Time: 25 minutes

Servings: 4

Ingredients

2 medium Russet potatoes, chopped roughly

Cooking spray

Pinch salt & red pepper flakes

1 small onion, chopped medium

1 small bell pepper, chopped medium

Preparation

1. Place the chopped potatoes in the fryer basket. Spray with cooking spray and then add salt and pepper.

2. Place the pressure cooker trivet in the inner steel pot. Place the basket on the trivet. Place the Crisp Lid on top of the inner pot and plug it in.

3. Cook 400°F at 10 minutes, shaking half way through.

4. Remove Crisp Lid, place on silicon mat and then add the onions and bell pepper to the potatoes in the basket. Spritz with oil. Return Crisp Lid and plug in.

5. Cook at 400°F for 15 minutes, shaking half way through cooking.

6. Serve, seasoned with salt.

Per Serving: Calories 81; Total Fat; Protein 3g; Total Carb 17g; Sodium: 12mg Fiber: 3g

Indian Bread/Potato Rolls

Prep Time: 20 minutes

Cook Time: 35 minutes

Servings: 2; 4 yields

Ingredients

3 medium potatoes

4 vegan bread slices

1 green chilies, seeded and chopped finely

1 tablespoon of finely chopped coriander

1 small onion, finely chopped

1/4 teaspoon turmeric

1/4 teaspoon of mustard seeds

1 sprigs curry leaf

1 teaspoon oil

Salt to taste

Preparation

1. Trim the brown sides of the vegan bread and discard. Mash potatoes and chop the seasonings.

2. Boil the potatoes with a spoon full of salt, peel and thoroughly mash them.

3. In your pressure cooker, sauté the mustard seed in a teaspoon of oil and then add the chopped onion and cook until translucent. Add the curry leaves and turmeric and stir for 5 seconds. Now add the salt, mix and turn off sauté function and pressure cooker. Transfer to a baking sheet to cool.

4. Shape mixture into 4 oval portions and set aside.

5. Wet bread slice fully with water and then press with the hand/ palm to remove excess water. Roll wet bread over the potato rolls, ensuring that all potato edges are sealed and that the potato filling is inside the bread completely.

6. Place all bread potato rolls in the fryer basket. Spray with cooking spray.

7. Cook at 400°F for 20 minutes until golden crisp. Enjoy with ginger tea.

Per Serving: Calories 455; Total Fat; 26g; Protein 7g; Total Carb 53g; Sodium: 273mg; Cholesterol: 61mg; Fiber: 4g

Vegan Casserole With Quinoa

An appetizing and flavorsome breakfast dish.

Prep time: 15 minutes

Cook time: 20 minutes

Servings: 2

Ingredients:

7 ounces of tofu, extra-firm

½ cup of cooked quinoa

½ cup of shiitake mushrooms, diced

½ cup of bell pepper, diced

2 tablespoons of water

2 tablespoons of plain soy yogurt

2 tablespoons of nutritional yeast

1 tablespoon of lemon juice

2 small celery stalks

1 small onion

1 large carrot

1 teaspoon of dried oregano

1 teaspoon of vegetable oil

1 teaspoon of garlic, minced

½ teaspoon of ground cumin

½ teaspoon of red pepper flakes

½ teaspoon of freeze-dried dill

½ tsp black pepper

½ tsp salt

Preparation

1. In your pressure cooker, sauté the garlic and onion in olive oil for 3 to 5 minutes until brown. Add the carrots, bell pepper and celery and sauté 3 minutes.

2. Add the red pepper flakes, the cumin, black pepper, dill, salt, oregano and the mushrooms. Stir to mix and lower heat.

3. In a food processor, pulse the yogurt, yeast, tofu, lemon juice and the water until creamy. Add to the pot and add the quinoa as well. Combine thoroughly. Turn off pressure cooker.

4. Turn the mixture into a pan. Place pan on trivet. Place the Crisp Lid on top of the inner pot and plug it in.

5. Set to 350°F for 15 minutes.

6. Remove and leave to rest for 5 minutes. Serve.

Per Serving: Calories 595; Total Fat; 31g; Protein 27g; Total Carb 52g; Sodium: 644mg; Cholesterol: 0mg; Fiber: 12g

ENTREES

Creamy Fried Lasagna

Lasagna noodle pockets filled with creamy tofu ricotta filled, coated in breadcrumbs and herbs and then air fried.

Prep Time: 25 minutes

Cook Time: 15 minutes

Servings: 2

Ingredients

6 lasagna pasta sheets

1/2 block extra firm tofu

2 garlic cloves

2 tablespoons of nutritional yeast

2 teaspoon canola oil

2 tablespoons of fresh lemon juice

Pinch of black pepper

1/2 tsp. salt

1 cup almond milk

1 cup bread crumbs, vegan

1 teaspoon of apple cider vinegar

1/2 tsp. oregano, dried

1/2 tsp. parsley, dried

1/2 tsp. garlic powder

Preparation

1. Boil the lasagna sheets as instructed on the package. Drain the boiled sheet and cool.

2. To make the ricotta, press tofu and then add the pressed tofu, garlic, the nutritional yeast, oil, lemon juice, the salt and the pepper in a processor and pulse until smooth.

3. Pat dry lasagna sheets if still wet, and then place on a plate. Spread out about 2 tablespoons of the ricotta mixture evenly on the sheet. Do this for all sheets.

4. In a bowl, combine the almond milk and the apple cider vinegar and mix. Let it sit for at least 1-2 minutes to curdle a bit.

5. Add the breadcrumbs to a separate bowl and add the dried herbs as well. Stir thoroughly to combine.

6. Dip a folded lasagna to the almond milk mix, and coat in the bread crumbs on all sides. Do this for all folded lasagnas.

7. Place 2 lasagna in the fryer basket, spritz with spray. Place the pressure cooker trivet in the inner steel pot. Place the basket on the trivet. Place the Crisp Lid on top of the inner pot and plug it in.

8. Cook at 400°F for 10 minutes. Halfway through cooking, flip. Cook until brown and crispy

9. Serve with marinara sauce. This recipe yields 6 lasagnas.

Lasagna With Pasta Sauce

This recipe is just for one. It includes creamy tofu ricotta, fresh basil and spinach, zucchini and jarred pasta sauce.

Prep Time: 20 minutes

Cook Time: 25 minutes

Servings: 1

Ingredients

2 lasagna egg-free noodles

Salt

1/4 cup tofu ricotta

1/2 cup pasta sauce

1 handful fresh basil leaves, chopped, chopped, (about 1/4 cup)

1 handful baby spinach leaves chopped, (about 1/4 cup)

3 tablespoons zucchini, shredded

Preparation

1. Break noodles in half.

2. Add water to pot and bring to boil. Add salt and boil noodles as instructed on the package, drain and pat dry with kitchen towel.

3. Line bottom of a mini loaf with 2 tablespoons of pasta sauce, add 1 tablespoon of tofu ricotta on top, pinch basil, pinch spinach and pinch zucchini. Ensure all is spread across the noodles evenly.

4. Add another noodle and top as before and then finish up with the last noodle, ensuring that noodles are thoroughly covered. Sprinkle tofu ricotta over.

5. Cover pan with aluminum foil. Place the pressure cooker trivet in the inner steel pot. Place the pan on the trivet. Place the Crisp Lid on top of the inner pot and plug it in.

6. Cook at 400°F for 10 minutes. Remove foil, cook 5-7 minutes, until crispy on top. Let it sit for a while, remove to a plate and enjoy.

Per Serving: Calories 344; Total Fat 9g; Protein 14g; Total Carb 52g; Sodium:843mg Fiber: 3g

Chewy Panko Tofu

You'll love this dish! It's so flavorful and tasty!

Prep Time: 10 minutes

Cook Time: 20 minutes

Servings: 4

Ingredients:

Tofu:

1 block extra firm tofu, pressed & drained

1 cup of panko breadcrumbs

½ cup vegan mayo

1 teaspoon of kosher salt

Marinade:

¼ cup of soy sauce

1 teaspoon of ground ginger

1 tablespoon of sesame oil, toasted

1 teaspoon rice vinegar

½ teaspoon garlic powder

Preparation

1. Press and drain tofu, then slice into 8 cutlets.

2. Mix the marinade ingredients in a bowl. In a shallow dish, place the cutlets and drizzle over with the marinade. Let it marinate for 30 minutes - 1 hour.

3. Now add the mayo to a shallow bowl. In a different bowl, add together the panko and salt

4. Dredge each cutlet in the mayo and then the panko mix. Place in the fryer basket evenly in one layer.

5. Cook at 375°F for 20 minutes, shaking halfway through cooking.

Per Serving: Calories 232; Total Fat 13g; Protein 13g; Total Carb 14g; Sodium:1249mg Fiber: 2g

Cauliflower steak with gravy

Cauliflower Steaks With Mushroom Cashew Gravy

A healthy and yummy southern comfort dish!

Prep Time: 20 minutes

Cook Time: 40 minutes

Servings: 4

Ingredients

Cauliflower Steaks:

1 whole cauliflower

1 cup water

1/2 cup of cashews, raw

1 tablespoon onion powder, divided

1 tablespoon garlic powder, divided

1 tablespoon lemon pepper divided

1/2 tablespoon &1 teaspoon smoked paprika

Salt to taste

1 cup of raw pumpkin seeds, unsalted (pepitas)

1 cup hemp seeds

Cooking spray

Mushroom Gravy:

1/2 cup of cashews

2 cups of water

1/2 vegetable bouillon cube

1/2 tablespoon mushroom seasoning, optional

1 tablespoon coconut oil

8 oz. mushrooms, sliced

2 tablespoons cracked black peppercorns

1 yellow onion, thinly sliced

Preparation

1. Begin by cutting the cauliflower into steaks. Once done, blend the cashews, and add in a shallow baking dish, together with ½ of the garlic, onion, smoked paprika, pepper, water and a sprinkle of salt.

2. Blend the pumpkin seeds and the hemp seeds in a food processor for about 12 seconds and the pour into a plate. Season with a teaspoon of paprika, salt and ½ tablespoon of garlic, onion and the lemon pepper.

3. Place the steaks on a large plate and then dip one at a time, into the cashew mixture to coat evenly. Dip also in the pumpkin/hemp seed mixture to coat evenly. Place on plate or baking pan. Coat any broken pieces of steak the same way and place on pan/ plate.

4. Transfer to the fryer basket, in batches, and spritz with cooking spray.

5. Place the pressure cooker trivet in the inner steel pot. Place the basket on the trivet. Place the Crisp Lid on top of the inner pot and plug it in.

6. Set temperature at 360°F and timer at 25 minutes, shaking halfway through.

7. Meanwhile, make the gravy. Blend the cashews, bouillon cube, mushroom seasoning (if using) until smooth.

8. Add the oil to a large pan and once hot, add the onions, mushrooms and peppercorns and cook 10 minutes until softened.

9. Add the cashew milk mixture and let it simmer. Lower heat, cover and let it simmer for 5 minutes. Turn off heat and add some water, if too thick.

10. Enjoy your crispy cauliflower steaks with a scoop of mushroom peppercorns gravy!

Per Serving: Calories 931; Total Fat 6g; Protein 35g; Total Carb 36g; Sodium:1046mg, Cholesterol:65mg; Fiber: 12g

Roasted Veggies Pasta Salad

Prep Time: 10 minutes

Cook Time: 15 minutes

Servings: 3-4

Ingredients:

1 ounce of brown mushrooms, cut in halves

½ pound of cooked rigatoni or penne rigate

½ cup of grape tomatoes, cut in halves

¼ cup of pitted Kalamata olives, cut in halves

Cooking spray

11/2 tablespoons of balsamic vinegar

1tablespoons of chopped fresh basil

1 small red onion, sliced

1 small green pepper, cut largely

1 small red pepper, cut into large chunks

1 small orange pepper, cut into large chunks

1 small zucchini, sliced in half moons

1 small yellow squash, sliced in half moons

Pinch Italian seasoning

Salt

Fresh ground black pepper

Preparation

1. Add the zucchini, peppers, red onion, yellow squash and mushrooms in a large bowl. Spritz lightly with oil. Toss to coat and season with the Italian seasoning, salt and pepper.

2. Place in the fryer basket, plug in the Crisp Lid and cook at 380°F for 15 minutes until veggies are mushy, not tender. Shake basket halfway through cooking.

3. In a large bowl, mix the roasted veggies, the pasta, olives and the tomatoes thoroughly. Toss with the balsamic vinegar and season with the salt and pepper.

4. Stir in the fresh basil and serve immediately.

Per Serving: Calories 391; Total Fat 26g; Protein 10g; Total Carb 58g; Sodium:334mg, Cholesterol:61mg; Fiber:3g

Crispy tofu

Quick & Easy Crispy Tofu

Crispy, firm and delicious! The perfect appetizer in just 30 minutes! Can also be a perfect side dish to a salad or a stir-fry. Enjoy!

Prep Time: 10 minutes

Cook Time: 20 minutes

Servings: 2

Ingredients

16 ounces extra firm tofu

1 pinch sea salt

1 teaspoon curry powder or chili powder

1 tablespoon coconut oil

Preparation

1. Wrap the tofu in an absorbent towel, press to remove excess water by setting something heavy on it. Unwrap, pat dry and remove to a bowl.

2. Drizzle oil over the tofu as well as the salt and seasoning.

3. Arrange in Crisp Lid fryer basket, in batches, and ensure it is placed in a single layer. Set the trivet in the pot of the pressure cooker. Place the fryer basket on the trivet and then set the Crisp lid on the pot and plug it in.

3. Set temperature to 350°F and cook for 10 minutes; flip tofu using tongs and continue cooking until crispy.

Per Serving: Calories 225; Total Fat 17g; Protein 18.6g; Total Carb 3.8g; Fiber:2g

Rebaked Stuffed Potatoes

Baked potato filled with a creamy mash and baked again. You can mix in any of your favorite herbs or spices and even a little shredded vegan cheese if you want.

Prep Time: 25minutes

Cook Time: 1 hr. 25minutes

Servings: 4

Ingredients

2 large Russet baking potatoes

Cooking spray

1/4 cup unsweetened nondairy milk

1/4 cup unsweetened vegan yogurt

2 tablespoons nutritional yeast

1/2 teaspoon salt substitute

1/4 teaspoon pepper

1 cup spinach or kale, chopped

For topping:

1/4 cup unsweetened vegan yogurt

Smoked salt and pepper

Chives parsley, chopped

Preparation

1. Spray potato with oil. Place on fryer basket. Place the pressure cooker trivet in the inner steel pot. Place the basket on the trivet. Place the Crisp Lid on top of the inner pot and plug it in.

2. Set at 390°F and cook for 30-40 minutes. Turn potato over and cook again for 30-40 minutes. Potato is cooked when it can be pierced easily with a fork. Cool the potatoes.

3. Once cooled, cut in half across the length, scoop out the center and then mash the scooped potato, along with the non-dairy milk, vegan yoghurt, nutritional yeast and the salt and pepper. Do this until smooth.

4. Now add the chopped spinach and fill the potato shells with it. Place all 4 in the fryer basket, or cook in batches, if necessary.

5. Cook at 375 for 5 minutes.

6. Serve with desired toppings.

Per Serving: Calories 399; Total Fat 2g; Protein 13g; Total Carb 84g; Sodium:954mg, Cholesterol:1mg; Fiber: 10g

Cauliflower Buffalo Wings With Cashew Cream Sauce

Prep Time: 20 minutes

Cook Time: 20 minutes

Servings: 4

Ingredients

Cauliflower:

1 small cauliflower, about 14 oz. florets

¼ cup flour

1½ tablespoons Sriracha

1½ tablespoons of white vinegar

1 teaspoon garlic powder

½ teaspoon smoked paprika

½ teaspoon sugar

1 teaspoon sea salt flakes

1 teaspoon oil

¼ cup of water

Cashew Cream Sauce:

1 cup raw cashew nuts

1 garlic clove

1 teaspoon lemon juice

½ teaspoon sea salt flakes

½ cup water

½ teaspoon nutritional yeast

Preparation

1. Prepare the cauliflower. Cut the cauliflower into big florets of about 2 inches wide at the head. Combine all ingredients in a large bowl, and mix to fully incorporate the florets.

2. Place in the fryer basket, working in batches. Place the pressure cooker trivet in the inner steel pot. Place the basket on the trivet. Place the Crisp Lid on top of the inner pot and plug it in.

3. Set temperature to 375°F, cook for 20 minutes.

4. In the meantime, prepare your cashew cream sauce. Soak the cashew nuts in boiling water for 10 to 15 minutes. Drain and transfer to a food processor. Add the rest of the ingredients. Pulse to smoothness.

5. Serve, cooked cauliflower wings, garnished with sour cashew cream sauce, greens, crushed peanuts and lemon wedges.

Per Serving: Calories 693; Total Fat 39g; Protein 12g; Total Carb 78g; Sodium:1391mg, Cholesterol:0mg; Fiber: 10g

Mashed Potato Dinner

Prep Time: 10 minutes

Cook Time: 20 minutes

Servings: 2-3

Ingredients

2 medium red potatoes, cut into pieces and cooked with the skin (If microwaving, cook and then cut).

1 tablespoon vegan margarine

1/4 cup unsweetened soy milk

Salt and black pepper, to taste

Tofu:

½ block extra firm tofu, pressed and cut into pieces (1")

½ teaspoon garlic powder

1 tablespoons soy sauce

Kale and Corn:

½ tablespoon olive oil

2 full cups of chopped kale

½ cup corn kernels, fresh or frozen

1 tablespoon seasoned rice vinegar

½ teaspoon garlic powder

Preparation

1. Cook the potatoes and mash in a bowl, together with the butter, until slightly lumpy. Add the soy milk and mash until desired consistency is attained. Set aside, covered.

2. Meanwhile, while the potatoes are cooking, place the tofu in a fryer basket, sprinkle the ginger powder and soy sauce to completely coat the tofu.

3. Place the pressure cooker trivet in the inner steel pot. Place the basket on the trivet. Place the Crisp Lid on top of the inner pot and plug it in.

4. Cook at 420F for 20 minutes, shaking halfway through.

5. Meanwhile, while the tofu cooks, Add oil to a pan and heat. Add the corn and kale and the garlic powder. Cook and stir for about 5 minutes until the kale is bright green in color and starts to wilt.

6. Now add the rice vinegar, stir to coat the vegetables, and cook another 2-3 minutes.

7. Divide mashed potatoes into bowls, add the kale/corn mix and then add the tofu. Additionally, add desired toppings like green onions, roasted cashews, and vegan mayo.

Per Serving: Calories 326; Total Fat 13g; Protein 12g; Total Carb 39g; Sodium:1892mg, Cholesterol:0mg; Fiber: 5g

Air Fried Tofu

Oil-Free Tofu In Lemon Sauce

Prep Time: 15 minutes

Cook Time: 25 minutes

Servings: 4

Ingredients

1 lb. extra-firm tofu, drained & then pressed

1 tablespoon of tamari

1 tablespoon cornstarch

For the sauce:

1/3 cup lemon juice

1 teaspoon lemon zest

1/2 cup of water

2 tablespoon sugar

2 teaspoons cornstarch

Preparation

1. Cut tofu in cubes and place in a sealable bag. Add tamari to it, seal and shake bag to coat the tofu with the tamari. Add the cornstarch and shake to coat tofu. Let it marinate for 20 minutes.

2. Combine in a small bowl; the rest of the ingredients and mix.

3. Place tofu in fryer basket, working in batches, and let it cook, with the Crisp Lid plugged at a temperature of 390°F for 10 minutes. Shake halfway through cooking.

4. Remove Crisp Lid, trivet and basket and plug in the pressure cooker. Add the cooked tofu to the inner pot, pour in the sauce and let it sauté and simmer with frequent stirring, until the sauce is thick and the tofu is well-heated.

5. Enjoy with rice and steamed veggies.

Per Serving: Calories 112; Total Fat 3g; Protein 8g; Total Carb 13g; Sodium:294mg

Baked Potato With Toppings

Absolutely yummy!

Prep Time: 10 minutes

Cook Time: 40 minutes

Servings: 1

Ingredients:

1 russet potato

Cooking spray

1/8 teaspoon of coarse salt

¼ teaspoon of onion powder

Optional toppings:

A dollop of vegan butter

A dollop of vegan cream

1 tablespoon of chopped chives

1 tablespoon sliced Kalamata olives

Salt

Pepper

Preparation

1. Poke holes into the potato with a knife and then rub the potato with the onion powder, oil and salt.

2. Place in fryer basket. Place the pressure cooker trivet in the inner steel pot. Place the basket on the trivet. Place the Crisp Lid on top of the inner pot and plug it in.

3. Cook at 390°F for 40 minutes, flipping halfway through.

4. Cut through the cooked potato and fill with your desired toppings.

Per Serving, minus toppings: Calories 134; Total Fat 2g; Protein 3g; Total Carb 28g; Sodium:293mg, Cholesterol:0mg; Fiber: 2g

Vegetable Kebab

Prep Time: 25 minutes

Cook Time: 10 minutes

Servings: 6-7 yields

Ingredients

½ cup chopped mixed vegetables of choice

1/4 cup tofu

1 medium boiled potatoes & then mashed

2 small green chilies

1 garlic cloves

½ -1 inch ginger

1/8 cup fresh mint leaves

1/4 teaspoon garam masala powder

1 tablespoons of corn flour

Salt to taste

1/2 tablespoons of chaat masala

Cooking spray

6-7 bamboo skewers

Preparation

1. Soak in bamboo skewers for 2- 3 hours. Cut your vegetables: chop, grate or mince depending on your chosen veggies. Afterwards, pulse the cut veggies, together with the garlic, ginger, green chilies, tofu and mint leaves in a food processor.

2. Combine the minced vegetables, corn flour, garam masala powder, mashed potatoes, and salt. Mix.

3. Roll into the 6-7 small balls, ensuring that the ends are firmly pressed. Spray with cooking spray.

4. Place in the fryer basket and cook at 375°F for 10 minutes.

5. Enjoy with salad and ketchup.

Per Serving: Calories 188; Total Fat 14g; Protein 3g; Total Carb 15g; Sodium:162mg, Cholesterol:35mg; Fiber: 4g

Flavored Cauliflower Stir-Fry

Nutrient dense, tasty and filling.

Prep Time: 5 minutes

Cook Time: 30 minutes

Servings: 4

Ingredients:

¾ cup of sliced onion

1 tablespoon of rice vinegar

1½ tablespoons of tamari

1 tablespoon of sriracha

Cooking spray

½ teaspoon of coconut sugar

1 head cauliflower

2 scallions, sliced

5 garlic cloves

Preparation

1. In your fryer basket, spray the cauliflower with oil/spray. Set on trivet and plug in Crisp Lid. Set at 360°F and cook for 20 minutes, shaking halfway through cooking.

2. Once cooked, remove Crisp Lid, place on silicon trivet, add the garlic, mix, return Crisp Lid and cook 5 more minutes.

3. Add the remaining ingredients in a small bowl. Do not add the scallions. Add to the cauliflower, stir and cook 5 minutes.

4. Finally, sprinkle the scallions over it and serve.

Per Serving: Calories 461; Total Fat 24g; Protein 9g; Total Carb 54g; Sodium:398mg; Cholesterol:0mg; Fiber: 9g

Orange Tofu

This is the ultimate tofu meal! An orange tofu dish, soft in the center but with crispy edges, tossed in a rich orange glaze.

Prep Time: 5 minutes

Cook Time: 15 minutes

Servings: 2

Ingredients

Tofu:

14 oz. block firm tofu

1 tablespoon tapioca

Kosher salt to taste

Orange Glaze:

4 tablespoons of orange juice

3 tablespoons of apple cider vinegar

2 tablespoons of soy sauce

2 tablespoons of almond butter

4 inch orange peel

Pinch red pepper flakes

Preparation

1. Drain the tofu, remove excess moisture with a towel, placing a pan on top. After 2-4 hours of draining moisture from tofu, tear into pieces with hands. Sprinkle the tapioca over it and salt. Toss to coat.

2. Line a fryer pan with parchment paper, place the tofu on it. Place on trivet and plug in Crisp Lid. Set at 400°F for 15 minutes, tossing halfway. Don't overcook. Remove immediately.

3. Meanwhile, while tofu is cooking, combine the orange glaze ingredients in a skillet and let it simmer on medium heat for 2-4 minutes until thick.

4. Add the cooked tofu to the orange glaze and toss to coat. Serve over rice or noodles and garnish dish with fresh chives, scallions or sesame seeds

Per Serving: Calories 323; Total Fat 17g; Protein 23g; Total Carb 19g; Sodium:1017mg

Stuffed Eggplant

Prep Time: 10 minutes

Cook Time: 10 minutes

Servings: 4

Ingredients:

10 small eggplant

¼ cup of vegan paneer, cut into pieces

1 tablespoons of tomato paste

1 onion, diced

1 tablespoon of oil

1 tomato, diced

A bunch of coriander leaves, diced

1 green bell pepper, diced

1 teaspoon of garlic, diced

1 teaspoon of pepper powder

A pinch of oregano

Salt

Preparation

1. Scoop out the center of eggplant and place in a bowl. Place empty eggplant in salty water so it doesn't get discolored.

2. Remove, place in the fryer basket, plug in Crisp Lid, set at 320°F and cook for 4-5 minutes.

3. Meanwhile, place oil in a pan and once hot, sauté the garlic and onions. Add the tomatoes, scooped eggplant mixture and salt. Let it sauté.

4. Add the oregano, paneer, bell pepper, pepper powder, coriander and the tomato paste. Mix well to combine.

5. Adjust seasoning. Fill the hollow eggplant with the stuffing mixture and close it with the cut out part of the eggplant.

6. Spray with cooking spray, place in the air fryer and cook at 356°F for 4-5 minutes.

Per Serving: Calories 587; Total Fat 28g; Protein 15g; Total Carb 79g; Sodium:235mg, Cholesterol:61mg; Fiber: 39g

SIDES

Vegan Cauliflower Gnocchi

Healthy, gluten-free and dairy free!

Prep Time: 5minutes

Cook Time: 15minutes

Servings: 4

Ingredients

1 bag of Trader Joe's Cauliflower Gnocchi

Preparation

1. Thaw content slightly. Microwave ingredient for about a minute. Flip to ensure it is thoroughly thawed.

2. Transfer to fryer basket. Place the trivet in the inner pot of your pressure cooker and place the basket on it. Place the Crisp-lid on top of the inner pot and plug in.

3. Cook at 400°F for 15 minutes, tossing half way through cooking. Enjoy with preferred sauce.

Per Serving: Calories 97; Total Fat: 1g; Protein 5g; Total Carb 19g; Sodium: 26mg Fiber: 4g

Sweet Potato Curry Fries With Cumin Dip

This amazing recipe adds some spice to your sweet potato dish.

Prep Time: 10 minutes

Cook Time: 20 minutes

Servings: 2

Ingredients

Fries:

2 small sweet potatoes

2 tablespoons of olive oil

¼ teaspoon of kosher salt

½ teaspoon of curry powder

¼ teaspoon of coriander

Cumin Dip:

¼ cup of ketchup

2 tablespoons of vegan mayo

½ teaspoon of ground cumin

A pinch of cinnamon

1/8 teaspoon of ginger, ground

Preparation

1. Cut the sweet potatoes into sticks of about ¼ inches. Place on a cookie sheet and drizzle with olive oil. Sprinkle the salt, coriander and the curry powder over it and then toss well to coat potatoes.

2. Transfer to the fryer basket. Place the pressure cooker trivet in the inner steel pot. Place the basket on the trivet. Place the Crisp Lid on top of the inner pot and plug it in.

3. Set at 370°F and cook for 20 minutes, tossing half way through cooking

4. In a small bowl, whisk all the ingredients for the dip together. Serve with the fries.

Per Serving: Calories 199; Total Fat 16g; Protein 3g; Total Carb 13g; Sodium:541mg, Cholesterol:0mg; Fiber: 1g

Crunchy Fish Taco Wrap With Mango Salsa

Prep Time: 50 minutes

Cook Time: 25 minutes

Servings: 4

Ingredients

4 large tortillas

1 small red bell pepper, cored, seeded, & then diced

1 small yellow onion, peeled & then diced

2 cobs fresh grilled corn

4 pieces fishless filet

1/3 cup Mango Salsa

Tortilla chips

Mixed greens (spinach, romaine, radicchio)

4 tablespoons shredded vegan cheese

Preparation

1. In your pressure cooker inner steel pot, sauté the onion and bell pepper for 5 minutes until soft. Add the grilled corn and cook for 2-3 more minutes. Remove to a bowl and cover. Turn off pressure cooker.

2. Place the fillets in the fryer basket. Place the pressure cooker trivet in the inner steel pot. Place the basket on the trivet. Place the Crisp Lid on top of the inner pot and plug it in. Cook at 400°F for 8 minutes. Remove Crisp Lid, place to cool on silicon mat.

3. Cut the cooked fillets into small pieces.

4. Now assemble the wrap. Scoop ¼ of the onion corn mix in the center of tortilla. Add pieces of the fillet, two tablespoons of the salsa, several tortilla

chips and then a handful of mixed greens. Fold the sides, and go round the circle of the tortilla to form a round wrap. To hold the tortilla together on all points, use 1 tablespoon of shredded cheese.

5. Now place side down on the fryer basket. Do this for all wraps, but you may have to work in batches.

6. Place the pressure cooker trivet in the inner steel pot. Place the basket on the trivet. Place the Crisp Lid on top of the inner pot and plug it in.

7. Cook at 350°F for 6 minutes.

Per Serving: Calories 375; Total Fat 17g; Protein 6g; Total Carb 53g; Sodium:442mg, Cholesterol:0mg; Fiber: 6g

Vermouth & Garlic Flavored Mushroom

Vermouth & Garlic Flavored Mushroom

Juicy, and flavorful!

Prep Time: 5 minutes

Cook Time: 30 minutes

Servings: 2

Ingredients

1 tablespoon of white vermouth

¼ teaspoon of garlic powder

1 pound mushrooms, washed & quartered

1 teaspoon of Herbes de Provence

1-2 tablespoons of olive oil

Preparation

1. Add the mushrooms to a bowl, add the rest of the ingredients and toss to coat the mushrooms.

2. Place in the fryer basket and air fry at 320°F for 15 minutes. Toss and cook again for 15 minutes.

Per Serving: Calories 92; Total Fat: 3.9g; Protein 7.2 g; Total Carb; 8.1g Sodium: 13mg; Fiber: 2.3g

Fried Vegan Ravioli

Prep Time: 15 minutes

Cook Time: 8 minutes

Servings: 4

Ingredients

1/2 cup of panko bread crumbs

1 teaspoon dried basil

2 teaspoons nutritional yeast flakes

1 teaspoon dried oregano

1 teaspoon garlic powder

Pinch salt & pepper

1/4 cup aquafaba liquid or vegan mayonnaise

8 ounces vegan ravioli

Cooking spray

1/2 cup of marinara for dipping

Preparation

1. Add together the panko bread crumbs, dried basil, nutritional yeast flakes, dried oregano, garlic powder, the salt, and the pepper.

2. Place the aquafaba in a small bowl.

3. Dip the ravioli first into the aquafaba, and then shake off excess liquid. Now dredge in bread crumb mixture and place in the fryer basket. Bread all the ravioli and cook in batches. Spritz with spray.

4. Cook at 390°F for 6 minutes. Flip and cook another 3 minutes. Remove and enjoy with marinara sauce.

Per Serving: Calories 150; Protein 5g; Total Carb; 27g Sodium: 41mg; Fiber: 2g

Roasted Asparagus

Prep Time: 2 minutes

Cook Time: 10 minutes

Servings: 4

Ingredients

1 lb. fresh asparagus

Dash of kosher salt

Dash of ground black pepper

Cooking spray

Preparation

1. Trim the ends of the asparagus an inch or so, from the bottom. Place in the fryer basket. Sprinkle salt and pepper and spray with cooking spray. Toss to coat.

2. Place the pressure cooker trivet in the inner steel pot. Place the basket on the trivet. Place the Crisp Lid on top of the inner pot and plug it in.

3. Set temperature to 400°F and cook for 7- 10 minutes.

4. Remove and serve.

Nutrition info for ¼ asparagus:

Per Serving: Calories 53; Total Fat 4g; Protein 3g; Total Car 4g; Fiber: 2g

Spicy Bok Choy

A delicious sides or snacks, made even more appealing with the added touch of ginger, garlic and Chile paste.

Prep Time: 15 minutes

Cook Time: 6 minutes

Servings: 2

Ingredients

1/8 cup grape seed oil

¼ teaspoon chile paste

½ teaspoon garlic, freshly grated

½ teaspoon ginger pulp

4 heads Baby Bok Choy

Sea salt

Dried chile flakes, for garnish

Preparation

1. Cut off the bottoms of the bok choy, separate the leaves, and then wash, shaking off excess water and then dry.

2. Add together the oil, garlic, ginger and chile paste in a bowl and mix to blend evenly.

3. Dredge the bok choy leaves through the mixture and place in the fryer basket. Place the pressure cooker trivet in the inner steel pot. Place the basket on the trivet. Place the Crisp Lid on top of the inner pot and plug it in.

4. Cook at 425°F for 6 minutes, flipping half way through cooking

5. Serve, sprinkled with dried chili flakes.

Per Serving: Calories 173; Total Fat 14g; Protein 4g; Total Carb 7g; Sodium:1254mg, Cholesterol:0mg; Fiber: 4g

Green Bean And Mushroom Bowl

A refreshingly light alternative to green bean casserole for any day!

Prep Time: 10 minutes

Cook Time: 12minutes

Servings: 3

Ingredients

12 oz. fresh green beans trimmed

1 cup sliced button mushrooms

1/2 fresh lemon juiced

½ tablespoon garlic powder

½ teaspoon ground sage

½ teaspoon onion powder

½ teaspoon salt

½ teaspoon black pepper

Spray oil

Preparation

1. Combine the green beans, the mushrooms, garlic powder, lemon juice, onion powder, sage, salt and pepper in a large bowl.

2. Place in the fryer basket. Spritz with oil. Place the pressure cooker trivet in the inner steel pot. Place the basket on the trivet. Place the Crisp Lid on top of the inner pot and plug it in.

3. Cook at 400°F for 12 minutes, shaking every 3 minutes.

Per Serving: Calories 66; Total Fat 1g; Protein 5g; Total Carb 12g; Sodium:399mg, Cholesterol:0mg; Fiber: 4g

Garlic Thyme Tomatoes

Prep Time: 8 minutes

Cook Time: 15 minutes

Servings: 4

Ingredients:

4 roma tomatoes

1 garlic clove, crushed

½ teaspoon of dried thyme

Salt

Freshly ground black pepper

Cooking spray

Preparation

1. Cut the tomatoes in half, remove the seeds and pith.

2. Place the ingredients in a bowl and toss to coat the tomatoes.

3. Place the tomatoes, with its sides up, in the fryer basket.

4. Plug Crisp Lid and cook at 390°F for 15 minutes or until the edges just starts to brown.

Per Serving: Calories 221; Total Fat 23g; Protein 1g; Total Carb 4g; Sodium:167mg, Cholesterol:61mg; Fiber: 1g

Sweet & Spicy Roasted Acorn Squash

A perfect side dish; healthy and delicious!

Prep Time: 5 minutes

Cook Time: 20 minutes

Servings: 2

Ingredients

1 small acorn squash

Cooking spray

1 tablespoon of brown sugar

½ teaspoon of cinnamon

1/8 teaspoon of ground cloves

2 tablespoon of pecans, chopped (optional)

Preparation

1. Cut the squash in half across the length, scrape out the seeds and discard. Spritz the flesh sides with oil.

2. Combine the cinnamon, sugar, cloves and pecan in a bowl and sprinkle on the squash.

3. Place the halves, with the cut side down on the fryer basket. Place the pressure cooker trivet in the inner steel pot. Place the basket on the trivet. Place the Crisp Lid on top of the inner pot and plug it in.

4. Cook at 375°F for 20 minutes

Nutrition info for half a squash:

Per Serving: Calories 210; Total Fat 9.5g; Protein 8g; Total Carb 31g; Sodium:10mg Fiber: 2.5g

Cauliflower Wings

Crispy on the outside, soft on the inside.

Prep Time: 10 minutes

Cook Time: 25minutes

Servings: 6

Ingredients

1 head of cauliflower florets

1/2 cup soy milk

1/2 cup water

3/4 cup all-purpose flour

1 teaspoon onion powder

2 teaspoon garlic powder

1 teaspoon smoked paprika

1/4 teaspoon ground black pepper

1/2 teaspoon salt

1 cup frank's red hot sauce

2 tablespoons Earth balance butter

1/4 cup molasses

Preparation

1. Whisk together all the dry ingredients in a bowl. Add the water and milk and whisk until it is lump-free.

2. Add the cauliflower florets and mix to coat with the batter. Remove florets and place in a separate bowl to run off excess batter.

3. Place the battered florets in the fryer basket. Do this in a single layer.

4. Cook at 350F for 15 minutes.

5. While it cooks, combine the vegan butter, hot sauce, and molasses in a small pot and let it simmer. A microwave can also be used.

6. Place the cooked cauliflower in a bowl and coat with sauce. Serve!

Per Serving: Calories 241; Total Fat: 7g; Protein 4g; Total Carb 40g; Sodium: 2165mg Fiber: 2g

Crispy Sweet Plantains
Enjoy this sweet treat with beans and rice or simply stuff it into a vegan taco!

Prep Time: 5minutes

Cook Time: 10minutes

Servings: 4

Ingredients

2 ripe plantains

Cooking spray

1/8 teaspoon salt

Preparation

1. Slice plantain to thick pieces of about 1/2".

2. Toss all the ingredients in a bowl, spritz generously with oil.

3. Transfer to fryer basket. Place the trivet in the inner pot of your pressure cooker and place the basket on it. Place the Crisp-lid on top of the inner pot and plug in.

4. Cook at 400°F for 10 minutes, tossing half way through cooking.

Per Serving: Calories 116; Total Fat: 0g; Protein 1g; Total Carb 31g; Sodium: 78mg; Fiber: 2g

Lemon Green Beans

Prep Time: 5minutes

Cook Time: 12 minutes

Servings: 4

Ingredients

1 lb. of green beans, washed and stemmed

1 lemon

Cooking spray

Salt

Black pepper

Preparation

1. Place the green beans in the fryer basket. Squeeze the lemon over it and sprinkle with a little salt and pepper.

2. Spritz with oil. Cook at 400°F for 12 minutes.

Per Serving: Calories 240; Total Fat: 23g; Protein 2g; Total Carb 9g; Sodium: 170mg; Fiber: 3g

APPETIZERS

Crispy Fried Beer Pickles

The crispy pickles are coated in beer batter, breaded in with panko and air fried in the Crisp Lid. The result is a crispy appetizer for your guests. Enjoy!

Prep Time: 15 minutes

Cook Time: 10minutes

Servings: 4

Ingredients

14 dill pickle slices, thickly cut

1/4 cup all-purpose flour

1/8 teaspoon baking powder

3 tablespoons of vegan All German dark beer

Pinch salt

2 tablespoons cornstarch

2 tablespoons water

6 tablespoons of panko bread crumbs

Pinch cayenne pepper

1/2 teaspoon paprika

Cooking spray

1/4 to vegan ranch dressing

Preparation

1. Dry the pickles and set aside.

2. Combine in a small bowl; the flour, baking powder, the beer, water and pinch of salt and mix until thick like waffle batter.

3. Place the cornstarch in a plate; in another, add together the panko bread crumbs, cayenne pepper, paprika, and a pinch of salt.

4. Dredge a pickle slice in cornstarch, shake off excess and then dip the slice in beer batter, ensuring it coats well. Drip off excess batter and dredge in the panko mixture.

5. Place in the fryer basket. Spritz with oil. Place the trivet in the inner pot of your pressure cooker and place the basket on it. Place the Crisp-lid on top of the inner pot and plug in.

6. Set at 360°F for 10 minutes, flipping and spritzing with spray half way through cooking.

7. Serve with vegan ranch dressing. Makes about 13-14 pickle slices.

Per Serving: Calories 111; Protein 3g; Total Carb 21g; Sodium: 325mg Fiber: 1g

Crispy Green Tomatoes
An elegant dish, made to impress!

Prep Time: 15 minutes

Cook Time: 7minutes

Servings: 2

Ingredients

1 cup soy milk

1 cup of panko bread crumbs

½ cup of flour, instant

2 large green tomatoes, cut thickly into ¼-inches

½ tablespoon of Creole seasoning

½ teaspoon of pepper

1 teaspoon of salt

Preparation

1. Place the thickly cut tomato slices on a plate and with the salt and pepper.

2. Place the flour in a plate. Pour the soy milk in a dish and in a third dish or plate, add together the panko crumbs and Creole seasoning.

3. Dredge the tomato first in the flour, dip it in in the soy milk and coat with the breadcrumbs on both sides.

4. Transfer to the fryer basket. Spray with cooking spray. Place the pressure cooker trivet in the inner steel pot. Place the basket on the trivet. Place the Crisp Lid on top of the inner pot and plug it in.

5. Cook the tomato at 400°F for 7 minutes.

Per Serving: Calories 331; Total Fat 4g; Protein 14g; Total Carb 64g; Sodium:2195mg, Cholesterol:0mg; Fiber: 6g

Roasted Broccoli
A really easy, fast and tasty dish!

Prep Time: 3minutes

Cook Time: 7 minutes

Servings: 2

Ingredients

2 cups fresh broccoli (about a pound), trimmed

Cooking spay

Sea salt & black pepper, to taste

Preparation

1. Place broccoli in basket and spritz with oil. Sprinkle with salt and pepper and toss to coat well.

2. Set the Crisp Lid trivet in the inner pot of your pressure cooker, place the fryer basket on top and set the Crisp lid on top of the inner pot. Plug in.

3. Cook 400°F for 7 minutes. Serve!

Per Serving: Calories 61; Total Fat 4g; Protein 3g; Total Carb 6; Fiber: 2g

Crispy Pickles

Nice and really crispy! But do not use coconut milk to prepare.

Prep Time: 15 minutes

Cook Time: 10 minutes

Servings: 4

Ingredients

1 1/2 cups dill pickle chips

1 cup all-purpose flour

1/2 cup plant-based milk

1 cups panko breadcrumbs

½ tablespoon ground cumin

1 teaspoon dried oregano

1 teaspoon smoked paprika

1/4 teaspoon ground black pepper

Salt to taste

Cooking spray

Preparation

1. Place pickles on paper towels and cover with paper towels to absorb the liquid. Let it sit for 15 minutes.

2. In the meantime, whisk together the flour, cumin, oregano, paprika, pepper and salt in a medium bowl.

3. Pour the milk in a bowl and in another bowl, the panko breadcrumbs.

4. Coat a pickle in the flour, dip it in the milk, and then coat in the breadcrumbs. Do this for all the pickles. Transfer to the fryer basket, working in batches. Spritz with cooking spray.

5. Place the pressure cooker trivet in the inner steel pot. Place the basket on the trivet. Place the Crisp Lid on top of the inner pot and plug it in.

6. Set to 400°F and cook for 10 minutes. Enjoy!

Per Serving: Calories 198; Total Fat 2g; Protein 7g; Total Carb 38g; Sodium:596mg Fiber: 3g

Grilled Corn

Prep Time: 3 minutes

Cook Time: 15 minutes

Servings: 2

Ingredients:

2 whole corn on cob

Olive oil

2 teaspoons of paprika powder

Preparation

1. Remove the husk and silk of the corn and rub with oil.

2. Sprinkle the paprika powder over it and rub with hands.

3. Place in the fryer basket, set the Crisp lid trivet in the inner pot of your pressure cooker, place the fryer basket on top and set the Crisp lid on top of the inner pot. Plug in.

4. Set at 400°F and cook the corn for 15 minutes.

Per Serving: Calories 146; Total Fat 8g; Protein 4g; Total Carb 21g; Sodium:2mg Fiber: 3g

Air Crisp Falafel

The Crisp Lid produces falafels that are crunchy on the outside, yet tender on the inside and with great taste!

Prep Time: 20 minutes

Cook Time: 20 minutes

Servings: 15

Ingredients

1 cup of dry garbanzo beans

3/4 cup of fresh parsley, flat-leafed

1 1/2 cups of fresh cilantro, stems off

1 small red onion, cut in 4

1 garlic clove

2 tbsp chickpea flour

1 tablespoon ground cumin

1 tablespoon of ground coriander

1 tablespoon sriracha sauce

Salt to taste

Ground black pepper to taste

1/4 teaspoon baking soda

1/2 teaspoon baking powder

Cooking spray

Preparation

1. Remove stems of parsley. Add chickpeas to plenty of water and soak for 24 hours. Rub soaked chickpeas to loosen and remove skins and then rinse and drain. Dry chickpeas on a large towel, well spread out.

2. In a food processor, add together the chickpeas, parsley, cilantro, onion and garlic and blend to a rough paste. Remove to a bowl.

3. Add the chickpea flour, cumin, coriander and sriracha and then season with salt and pepper. Mix, cover bowl and leave to sit for an hour.

4. Now add baking soda and baking powder to the mixture and form 15 balls of equal sizes. Spray with cooking spray.

5. Place 7 falafel balls in the fryer basket. Place the pressure cooker trivet in the inner steel pot. Place the basket on the trivet. Place the Crisp Lid on top of the inner pot and plug it in.

6. Cook at a temperature of 375°F for 15 minutes, flipping halfway through cooking. Transfer to a plate and cook remaining falafels.

Per Serving: Calories 60; Total Fat 1.1g; Protein 3.1g; Total Carb 9.9g; Sodium:98mg Fiber: 2.9g

Onion Rings

Fat-free, easy, crispy and delicious!

Prep Time: 15 minutes

Cook Time: 10 minutes

Servings: 3

Ingredients

1 large yellow onion

Wet Mix:

1/4 cup flour

1/3 cup unsweetened plant milk of choice

1/4 teaspoon paprika

Dash turmeric

1/4 teaspoons salt

Dry Mix:

1/2 cup vegan panko bread crumbs

1/4 teaspoon paprika

Dash turmeric

Dash salt

Preparation

1. Slice onion end off and peel off outer skin and then cut into circular portions of about ½ inch. Now form a hollow ring by pressing the center of the onion from two of the onion layers. Do this for all onion portions

2. Add together all the ingredients in a bowl for the wet mix and stir to combine. In another bowl, add together all the ingredients for the dry mix and stir to combine. Better still, divide the dry mix ingredients in 2 bowls to make it more useable.

3. Dip the onion ring in the wet mix and then the dry and coat with the breadcrumbs.

4. Place in the fryer basket, set the Crisp lid trivet in the inner pot of your pressure cooker, place the fryer basket on top and set the Crisp lid on top of the inner pot. Plug in.

5. Cook at 400°F for 10 minutes. Serve warm.

Per Serving: Calories 108; Total Fat 1g; Protein 4g; Total Carb 23g; Sodium:284mg; Fiber: 0g

Crunchy Buffalo Cauliflower

Prep Time: 5 minutes

Cook Time: 20 minutes

Servings: 4

Ingredients

1 medium head cauliflower, chopped into florets (about 6 cups)

2 tablespoons Frank's Red Hot Sauce

1 1/2 teaspoons of maple syrup

2 teaspoons avocado oil

3 tablespoons nutritional yeast

1/4 teaspoon kosher salt

1 tablespoon cornstarch

Preparation

1. In a large bowl, combine all the ingredients, except the cauliflower. Whisk and then add the cauliflower, tossing to ensure an even coating.

2. Transfer half of it to the fryer basket. Place the pressure cooker trivet in the inner steel pot. Place the basket on the trivet. Place the Crisp Lid on top of the inner pot and plug it in.

3. Cook at 360°F for 15 minutes, shaking half way through. Remove Crisp Lid, place on silicon mat and then transfer cooked veggies to a plate. Add the remaining to basket. Plug in Crisp Lid and cook for 10 minutes.

4, Enjoy or refrigerate in the refrigerator for later use. To reheat, return to inner pot, plug in Crisp Lid and warm for 2 minutes.

Per Serving: Calories 87; Total Fat 3g; Protein 5g; Total Carb 12g; Sodium:356mg; Fiber: 4g

Cubed Butternut Squash

Prep Time: 10 minutes

Cook Time: 20 minutes

Servings: 4

Ingredients

1 small butternut squash

2 tablespoons oil

1/2 teaspoon paprika

1/2 teaspoon garlic powder

Kosher salt to taste

Black pepper, to taste

Preparation

1. Peel and cut the squash into small cubes of about ½ inches.

2. Add together in a bowl; the paprika, the garlic powder, oil, salt and pepper. Add the cubed squash and coat in the marinade.

3. Transfer to fryer basket, working in batches, if necessary.

4. Place the pressure cooker trivet in the inner steel pot. Place the pan on the trivet. Place the Crisp Lid on top of the inner pot and plug it in.

5. Set to 380°F and cook for 20 minutes, shaking half way through and cooking until tender.

Per Serving: Calories 218; Total Fat 7g; Protein 2g; Total Carb 41g; Sodium:392mg; Fiber: 5g

Low Carb Vegetable Kebabs
So simple to make!

Prep Time: 10 minutes

Cook Time: 10 minutes

Servings: 3

Ingredients

2 bell peppers

1 eggplant

1 zucchini

1/2 onion

Salt and black pepper to taste

6-inch skewers

Preparation

1. Cut the vegetables to 1 inch pieces and thread on skewers. Sprinkle salt and pepper over it.

2. Place in the fryer basket. Place the pressure cooker trivet in the inner steel pot. Place the basket on the trivet. Place the Crisp Lid on top of the inner pot and plug it in.

3. Set at 390°F and cook for 10-12 minutes.

Per Serving: Calories 81; Protein 3g; Total Carb 17g; Sodium: 12mg Fiber: 7g

Roasted Carrots with Thyme & Parsley

Prep Time: 10 minutes

Cook Time: 20 minutes

Servings: 4

Ingredients

1 pound carrots

1 1/2 tablespoons olive oil

1/2 teaspoon dried oregano

1/2 teaspoon dried thyme

1 1/2 tablespoons dried parsley

Salt & pepper

Preparation

1. Peel the carrots, slice in half and then slice again in half.

2. Place in the fryer basket, add the oil, oregano, thyme, parsley and a sprinkle of salt and pepper.

3. Place basket on trivet and plug in Crisp Lid. Cook 400°F for 20 minutes, flipping after 10 minutes of cooking

4. *Serve!*

Per Serving: Calories 217; Total Fat 19g; Protein 2g; Total Carb 12g; Sodium:159mg; Fiber: 4g

Crispy Fried Okra
Tastiest Okra ever!

Prep Time: 10 minutes

Cook Time: 10 minutes

Servings: 4

Ingredients

1/2 lb. okra

1/4 teaspoon turmeric

1/2 teaspoon cumin seeds

1 tablespoon coriander powder

1/2 teaspoon mango powder

1 teaspoon red chili flakes

1 teaspoon salt

2 tablespoons chickpea flour

1 teaspoon of chat masala

Cooking Spray

Preparation

1. Wash the okra and dry thoroughly. Once completely dried, cut into sticks.

2. Combine all the flour and spices ingredients in a mixing bowl and toss in the okra to coat well.

3. Place in the fryer basket. Spritz with oil. Place the pressure cooker trivet in the inner steel pot. Place the basket on the trivet. Place the Crisp Lid on top of the inner pot and plug it in.

4. Cook at 360°F for 10 minutes, flipping halfway. Serve, drizzled with freshly squeezed lemon juice, if desired.

Per Serving: Calories 37; Total Fat 1g; Protein 2g; Total Carb 7g; Sodium:591mg; Fiber: 2g

Whiskey Garlic Tofu

Prep Time: 20minutes

Cook Time: 10 minutes

Servings: 3

Ingredients

1/4 cup whiskey

1/4 cup vegan sugar (maple, coconut)

2 garlic cloves, peeled & minced

1 tablespoon apple cider vinegar

1 teaspoon onion powder

Sea salt & black pepper

1 block extra firm tofu, pressed

Preparation

1. Press tofu and slice into slabs of ½ inches.

2. In a saucepan, add together the sugar, garlic, whiskey and onion powder and vinegar. Stir and let it come to a boil. Simmer and stir 10 minutes. Remove from heat and let it cool.

3. Once cooled, coat the tofu slices in it and place on fryer basket, lined with parchment paper.

4. Place the pressure cooker trivet in the inner steel pot. Place the basket on the trivet. Place the Crisp Lid on top of the inner pot and plug it in.

5. Set temperature at 370F and timer for 10 minutes, flipping halfway through cooking.

Per Serving: Calories 250; Total Fat 7g; Protein 14g; Total Carb 22g; Sodium:33mg; Fiber: 2g

SNACKS

Keto Shishito Peppers

Gather friends together for a healthy snack; better still, enjoy a cool evening of crunchy Shishito Peppers and a sparkling glass of wine with your loved one. So cool!

Prep Time: 5 minutes

Cook Time: 10 minutes

Servings: 4

Ingredients

1 6 oz. bag of Shishito peppers

Salt & pepper to taste

Cooking spray

1/3 cup vegan cheese, grated

Lime

Preparation

1. Rinse the pepper and dry with paper towel. Transfer to a bowl, spritz with oil, and season with salt, and pepper.

2. Remove to fryer basket. Place the pressure cooker trivet in the inner steel pot. Place the basket on the trivet. Place the Crisp Lid on top of the inner pot and plug it in.

3. Cook at 350F for 10 minutes. Drizzle with lime juice, top with cheese and serve.

Per Serving: Calories 49; Total Fat 2g; Protein 1g; Total Carb 7g; Sodium:160mg; Fiber: 2g

Roasted Almonds

It's time for some quick snack!

Prep Time: 5 minutes

Cook Time: 10 minutes

Servings: 4

Ingredients

1 cup almonds

Cooking spray

½ teaspoon of salt

Preparation

1. Spread almond in basket and plug in Crisp Lid. Set to cook at 320°F for 10 minutes.

2. Remove, pour into a bowl. Spray with cooking spray, add salt and mix. Return to fryer basket.

3. Cook at 320°F for 3 minutes. Let it cool for 5 minutes. Enjoy!

Per Serving: Calories 133; Total Fat 11g; Protein 5g; Total Carb 5g; Sodium:291mg; Fiber: 3g

Crunchy Croutons

An easy 2- ingredient snacks.

Prep Time: 3 minutes

Cook Time: 8 minutes

Servings: 9

Ingredients:

2 slices of whole meal bread

Cooking spray

Preparation

1. Cut the bread into medium chunks and then place in the fryer basket. Spay with cooking spray.

2. Place the trivet in the inner pot of your pressure cooker and place the basket on it. Place the Crisp-lid on top of the inner pot and plug in.

3. Cook on 395°F for 8 minutes.

Bow Tie Pasta Chips

Crunchy and cute!

Prep Time: 10 minutes

Cook Time: 10 minutes

Servings: 2 cups

Ingredients

2 cups of dry whole wheat bow tie pasta

1 tablespoon of canola oil

1 tablespoon of nutritional yeast

1 1/2 teaspoon of Italian Seasoning Blend

1/2 teaspoon salt

Preparation

1. Cook the pasta halfway and drain. Add the oil, nutritional yeast, the Italian seasoning, and the salt and toss to mix.

2. Transfer to fryer basket, working in batches. Place the trivet in the inner pot of your pressure cooker and place the basket on it. Place the Crisp-lid on top of the inner pot and plug in.

3. Cook on 390°F for 5 minutes, shaking halfway through cooking. Cool. It gets crispier when cooled.

Nutritional info *4g per serving*

Per Serving: Calories 294; Protein 10g; Fat: 8g; Total Carb 49g; Sodium: 587mg Fiber: 2g

Bowtie pasta chips

Indian Beetroot Chips

A good way to enjoy beets!

Prep Time: 10 minutes

Cook Time: 25 minutes

Servings: 4

Ingredients

2 medium beetroot

Cooking spray

Salt & pepper to taste

Preparation

1. Wash the beetroot, peel skin and slice thinly. Spread slices on paper towel and place on top as well for 10 minutes to absorb any moisture.

2. Spritz with oil. Sprinkle with salt and place in the fryer basket. Place the trivet in the inner pot of your pressure cooker and place the basket on it. Place the Crisp-lid on top of the inner pot and plug in.

3. Set to 320°F and cook for 25 minutes, shaking halfway and then shaking every 5 minutes.

4. Remove crispy beets and season with salt and pepper. *Enjoy!*

Per Serving: Calories 18; Protein 1g; Fat: 0g; Total Carb 4g; Sodium: 105mg Fiber: 1g

Air Fried Baby Carrots

Prep Time: 5 minutes

Cook Time: 20 minutes

Servings: 4

Ingredients

1 lb. bag of baby carrots

Cooking spray

Salt & pepper

Preparation

1. Rinse carrots, pat dry and place in the fryer basket. Spray with cooking spray. Sprinkle lightly with salt and pepper.

2. Place the trivet in the inner pot of your pressure cooker and place the basket on it. Place the Crisp-lid on top of the inner pot and plug in

3. Set at 400°F and cook for 10 minutes. Stir carrots, Spritz with oil, season with salt and pepper, plug in Crisp Lid again and cook 10 more minutes.

Per Serving: Calories 40; Protein 1g; Fat: 0g; Total Carb 0g; Sodium: 161mg Fiber: 3g

Toasty Pecan
Low Carb and yummy!

Prep Time: 2 minutes

Cook Time: 10 minutes

Servings:

Ingredients

1 cup pecan halves

Cooking spray

1 teaspoon of pink Himalayan salt

Preparation

1. Season the pecan halves with salt, spritz with cooking spray and toss.

2. Place in the fryer basket and let it cook for 390F for 10 minutes, tossing every 3 to 4 minutes.

3. Remove and enjoy!

Per Serving: ½ cup Calories 201; Protein 3g; Fat: 21g; Total Carb 1g;

Roasted Chickpeas

Prep Time: 5 minutes

Cook Time: 21 minutes

Serving: 2

Ingredients

1 can chickpeas (no sugar added)

Cooking spray

1 teaspoon ground cumin

1 teaspoon ground coriander

1 teaspoon garlic powder

1/8 teaspoon ground ginger

Preparation

1. Drain and rinse the chickpeas and place in a bowl, together with the rest of the ingredients.

2. Stir well so that the oil and spices coat the beans well.

3. Place in the air fryer basket, on trivet, plug Crisp Lid and cook at 12 minutes for 370°F.

4. When time elapses, remove Crisp Lid, place on silicon mat and stir the beans, place back in and cook another 8 minutes at the same temperature. Stir again and cook an additional 1 minute.

5. Pack in bags and refrigerate until ready to eat them. Store for up to one week but roast again for 1-2 minutes to retain their crunchiness after a few days in the fridge. *Enjoy!*

Per Serving: Calories 200; Protein 10g; Fat: 5g; Total Carb 32g; Sodium: 441mg Fiber: 7

Chili Lime Roasted Cashew

Prep Time: 5minutes

Cook Time: 10 minutes

Servings: 4

Ingredients

1 cup cashew

1 t tablespoon of lime juice

1 teaspoon red chili powder

1 teaspoon salt

1 teaspoon pepper powder

Preparation

1. Rinse cashews with water, drain and place in a bowl.

2. Combine the lime juice, pepper powder, chili powder and salt and then toss together. Let it rest 5 minutes.

3. Remove to the fryer basket, place on trivet and plug in Crisp Lid. Set to 320°F and cook for 5 minutes. Let it cool.

4. Store the browned cashew nuts in an airtight container and serve

Per Serving: Calories 182; Protein 6g; Fat: 14g; Total Carb 10g; Sodium: 617mg Fiber: 1g

Easy Crunchy Kale Chips

Vitamin- packed kale is a great way to enjoy a crunchy snack, and at the same time, giving your health a significant boost.

Prep Time: 3 minutes

Cook Time: 3 minutes

Servings: 2

Ingredients

1 kale head

Cooking spray

1 teaspoon soya sauce

Preparation

1. Prepare the kale by removing its centre steam and then tearing it up into pieces of about 11/2 inches.

2. Wash them clean and dry and then toss with the soya sauce and spray with cooking spray.

3. Place in the fryer basket, plug in Crisp Lid and cook for 3 minutes at 392°F. Toss the leaves half way through. Serve and enjoy!

Per Serving: Calories 2; Protein 3g; Fat: 1g; Total Carb 6g; Sodium: 171mg Fiber: 2g

Kale/ Potato Nuggets

A nutritious and, tasty snack that can be prepared with leftover mashed potatoes.

Prep Time: 20minutes

Cook Time: 20minutes

Servings: 2

Ingredients

1 cup potatoes, finely chopped

1 teaspoon of canola oil

1 clove garlic minced

2 cups loosely packed kale, coarsely chopped

1/tablespoon of almond milk

Pinch sea salt

Pinch ground black pepper

Cooking spray

Preparation

1. Cook the potatoes until tender.

2. Meanwhile, in your pressure cooker, sauté the garlic in hot oil until brown; add the kale and sauté for a minute or two. Remove to a bowl. Wipe the inner pot dry.

3. Transfer the cooked potatoes to a bowl. Add the milk, the salt and pepper and mash. Place the mashed potatoes in a large bowl and add the cooked kale to it.

4. Roll the kale/potatoes mix into nuggets. Spray with cooking spray and place in the fryer basket. Place the pressure cooker trivet in the inner steel

pot. Place the basket on the trivet. Place the Crisp Lid on top of the inner pot and plug it in.

5. Set temperature to 390°F and cook for 15 minutes, shaking halfway through.

Per Serving: Calories 133; Total Fat 3g; Protein 5g; Total Carb 25g; Sodium:107mg Fiber: 4g

Kale chips

Cinnamon Roasted Apples

Prep Time: 5 minutes

Cook Time: 15 minutes

Servings: 4

Ingredients

4 sweet/tart apples

½ teaspoon ground cinnamon

Cooking spray

Preparation

1. Peel the apples, core and chop into pieces.

2. Spray fryer basket with cooking spray and place the apples in. Sprinkle with cinnamon and toss.

3. Place the trivet in the inner pot of your pressure cooker and place the basket on it. Place the Crisp-lid on top of the inner pot and plug in.

4. Cook at 400°F for 15, tossing half way through cooking.

5. Remove once browned and store, covered in a lid.

Per Serving: Calories 81; Protein 0g; Fat: 0g; Total Carb 22g; Sodium: 0mg Fiber: 5g

Savory Rosemary Cashews

Sweet and savory snack!

Prep Time: 2 minutes

Cook Time: 16 minutes

Servings: 4

Ingredients

½ lb. cashews

½ tablespoon of oil

½ teaspoon Worcestershire Sauce

1 tablespoon of rosemary

1/4 teaspoon mustard powder

1/4 teaspoon chili powder

1 teaspoon brown sugar

Preparation

1. Combine all the ingredients, (set aside the cashews) in a bowl. Mix well and pour onto the cashews in a separate bowl. Toss to coat.

2. Transfer to fryer basket, place on trivet and plug in Crisp Lid.

3. Cook at 320°F for 5 minutes. Remove Crisp Lid and place on silicon mat. Stir nuts and return Crisp Lid. Cook again for 10 minutes, shaking halfway as well.

4. Once golden, remove, spread out to cool on paper-lined cookies sheet. Enjoy or store in an airtight container for a week!

Per Serving: Calories 332; Protein 10g; Fat: 27g; Total Carb 18g; Sodium: 28mg Fiber: 2g

Vegan Cashew Bacon

Prep Time: 3 minutes

Cook Time: 10 minutes

Servings: 3

Ingredients:

1 1/2 cups of cashews, raw

1 tablespoons blackstrap molasses

1 1/2 tablespoons of liquid smoke

1 teaspoons of salt

Preparation

1. Place all the ingredients in a bowl and toss thoroughly to coat cashews evenly.

2. Place in the fryer basket, place on trivet and plug in Crisp Lid.

3. Set temperature to 350°F and cook for 10 minutes. Shake every 3 minutes.

Per Serving: Calories 455; Protein 14g; Fat: 35g; Total Carb 28g; Sodium: 843mg Fiber: 3g

Crunchy Sweet Potato Fries

A perfect snack that is guilt- free and perfect healthy!

Prep Time: 65 minutes

Cook Time: 20 minutes

Servings: 3

Ingredients

1 large sweet potato, peeled and cut

3/4 tablespoon corn starch

½ tablespoon canola oil

½ tablespoon olive oil

1 teaspoon paprika

1 teaspoon garlic powder

Salt and pepper to taste

Preparation

1. Soak the sweet potatoes in cold water for 1 hour.

2. Drain, place potatoes and cornstarch in a ziploc bag, seal and shake for even coating.

3. Spread potatoes out and coat with oil and seasonings Transfer to a fryer basket. Place on and plug in Crisp Lid.

4. Set to 380F and cook 25 minutes. Shake every 10 minutes. Once crispy, let it cool and then serve.

Per Serving: Calories 53; Protein 0g; Fat: 5g; Total Carb 3g; Sodium: 93mg Fiber: 0g

Crispy Salty Potato Peels

The perfect inexpensive snack!

Prep Time: 8 minutes

Cook Time: 10 minutes

Servings: 1

Ingredients

Peels from 4 medium-sized russet potatoes

Cooking spray

Pinch salt

Preparation

1. Place the potato peels in the fryer basket, working in batches if necessary. Spray with cooking and sprinkle over with salt.

2. Place the pressure cooker trivet in the inner steel pot. Place the basket on the trivet. Place the Crisp Lid on top of the inner pot and plug it in. Cook at 400°F for 8-10 minutes, shaking half way through cooking

3. Once browned and crispy, remove and serve with desired toppings.

Per Serving: Calories 60; Total Fat 9.5g; Protein 2g; Total Carb 13g; Sodium:10mg Fiber: 2g

Fried Green Tomatoes With Panko Coating

Prep Time: 15 minutes

Cook Time: 10 minutes

Servings: 2

Ingredients

1/2 cup panko bread crumbs

3 tablespoons of cornstarch

1/4 cup of vegan mayonnaise

1/2 teaspoon dried oregano

1/2 teaspoon dried basil

1/2 teaspoon granulated onion

Pinch salt & pepper

1 medium green tomato

Cooking spray

Preparation

1. Remove top stem of tomato, discard and slice the tomatoes thinly.

2. Place the cornstarch in one plate. In another, the vegan mayonnaise and in a third, the panko breadcrumbs.

3. Add the dried oregano, basil, granulated onion, the salt and pepper to the crumbs in the plate and mix thoroughly.

4. Dry tomato slices with a clean towel and then dip into the cornstarch to coat, shaking off excess and dip in the vegan mayonnaise. Ensure to coat well and shake off excess. Dredge in the crumb mix, covering well.

4. Place in the fryer basket and spritz with cooking spray. Place the pressure cooker trivet in the inner steel pot. Place the basket on the trivet. Place the Crisp Lid on top of the inner pot and plug it in.

5. Cook at 400°F for 7 minutes. Remove Crisp Lid, place on silicon mat, shake/ flip green tomatoes, spritz with cooking spray. Cook for 3 minutes.

6. Serve, sprinkled with a little salt.

Per Serving: Calories 358; Total Fat 25g; Protein 2g; Total Carb 27g; Sodium:271mg Fiber: 1g

Kale potato nuggets

DESSERTS

Vanilla Bean Cake

Prep Time: 10minutes

Cook Time: 10minutes

Servings: 2

Ingredients

1½ cup of flour

¾ cup of sugar

1 teaspoon of salt

1 teaspoon of baking soda

1 teaspoon of vanilla extract

¼ cup of vegetable oil

1 cup of water

Preparation

1. Add together all the ingredients and mix well.

2. Spray the fryer basket or pan with cooking spray and then pour the batter into it.

3. Place the pressure cooker trivet in the inner steel pot. Place the basket on the trivet. Place the Crisp Lid on top of the inner pot and plug it in.

4. Set at 330F and cook for 30 minutes. Let it cool slightly and then enjoy!

Per Serving: Calories 878; Total Fat 29g; Protein 10g; Total Carb 147g; Sodium:1800mg Fiber: 3g

Blackberry Apricot Crumble

Easy, yummy and healthy!

Prep Time: 10 minutes

Cooking Time: 20 minutes

Servings: 3-4

Ingredients

3½ oz. fresh blackberries

9 ounces of fresh apricots, halved, stone removed and cut into cubes

1/2 cup of flour

¼ cup of sugar

2 1/2 tablespoons of cold butter, vegan

1 tablespoon of lemon juice

Salt

Preparation

1. Add together the blackberries, apricots, 2 tablespoons of sugar and lemon juice in a bowl.

2. Transfer this mixture into an oven dish and spread it out.

3. In another bowl, combine the flour with the salt and left over sugar. Add the butter and a tablespoon of cold water. Using your fingertips, rub until the mixture is crumbly.

4. Preheat air fryer to 390°F.

5. Spread the flour mixture over the fruit evenly and press it down lightly.

6. Place the oven dish in the air fryer basket and cook for 20 minutes or until it turns golden.

Per Serving: Calories 878; Total Fat 29g; Protein 10g; Total Carb 147g; Sodium:1800mg Fiber: 3

Vegan Carrot Cake
A delicious one-serving dessert you'll definitely try again.

Prep Time: 10 minutes

Cook Time: 20 minutes

Servings: 1

Ingredients

1/4 cup whole wheat pastry flour

1 tablespoon sweetener

1/4 teaspoon baking powder

1/8 teaspoon ground dried ginger

1/4 teaspoon ground cinnamon

Pinch ground cloves

Pinch ground allspice

2 teaspoons unsweetened nondairy milk

2 tablespoons unsweetened nondairy milk plus

2 tablespoons carrot, grated

2 tablespoons walnuts, chopped

1 tablespoon raisins

1-2 teaspoons mild oil

Preparation

1. In a small round baking pan, add together the flour, the baking powder, sweetener, ginger, cinnamon, allspice and cloves and mix thoroughly with a fork for even distribution.

2. Now add the milk, walnuts, carrots, raison and oil and mix well.

3. Place the pressure cooker trivet in the inner steel pot. Place the pan on the trivet. Place the Crisp Lid on top of the inner pot and plug it in. Set to 350°F and cook for 20 minutes. Insert a fork to ensure the center is cooked.

4. Enjoy, if desired, with a homemade cream cheese topping. To make, whip 1 tablespoon of vegan cream cheese and powdered sugar together. Top cake with it and enjoy!

Per Serving: Calories 220; Total Fat 5g; Protein 4g; Total Carb 42g; Sodium: 47mg Fiber: 3g

Glazed Donuts

Prep Time: 10 minutes

Cook Time: 5 minutes

Servings: 4

Ingredients

1 can of 8-oz croissant dough, refrigerated

1 can 16-oz vanilla frosting

Preparation

1. Slice the dough into rounds of 1-inch and then open a hole in the center.

2. Transfer to fryer basket, spray with cooking spray. Plug in Crisp Lid and bake at 400° for 5 minutes, flipping halfway.

3. Transfer baked donuts to a paper plate.

4. Heat the frosting in a microwave for 30 seconds and drizzle on the donuts. Enjoy!

Per Serving: Calories 747; Total Fat 32g; Protein 14g; Total Carb 103g; Sodium: 1093mg Fiber: 4g

Pineapple Sticks With Yoghurt Dip
Incredibly delicious and easy to make.

Prep Time: 10 minutes

Cook Time: 10 minutes

Servings: 4

Ingredients:

Pineapple Sticks:

Half of 1 pineapple

¼ cup desiccated coconut

Yoghurt Dip:

1 cup of vegan vanilla yoghurt

1 small sprig of fresh mint, finely diced

Preparation

1. Cut the pineapple into chip-size sticks. Dice your fresh mint as well.

2. Dip the pineapple sticks into the desiccated coconut. Place in the fryer basket. Place the pressure cooker trivet in the inner steel pot. Place the pan on the trivet. Place the Crisp Lid on top of the inner pot and plug it in.

3. Set to 392°F for 10 minutes.

4. Combine the mint and vanilla yogurt in a bowl, stirring well to mix..

5. Serve pineapple sticks with the dip.

Per Serving: Calories 128; Total Fat 3g; Protein 10g; Total Carb 16g; Sodium: 182mg Fiber: 3g

Coconut Pineapples & Yoghurt Dip

Prep Time: 10 minutes

Cook Time: 10 minutes

Servings: 4

Ingredients

2 oz. dried coconut flakes

1 sprig of mint, finely chopped

8 oz. of vanilla yogurt

½ medium pineapple

Preparation

1. Cut the pineapple into chip-size sticks. Dip into the diced coconut and ensure it sticks to them.

2. Place the sticks in the fryer basket and cook for about 10 minutes.

4. Stir the mint leaves into the vanilla yogurt. Serve with pineapple sticks.

Heat the airfryer to 390°F.

Per Serving: Calories 80; Total Fat 5g; Protein 2g; Total Carb 7g; Sodium: 18mg Fiber: 0g

Apple/ Berries Crumble

A simple and pleasant way to enjoy a nice dessert.

Prep Time: 15 minutes

Cook Time: 20 minutes

Servings: 2

Ingredients

1 medium apple, diced finely

1/2 cup frozen blueberries or strawberries

1/4 cup + 1 tablespoon brown rice flour

1/2 teaspoon ground cinnamon

2 tablespoons of sugar

2 tablespoons nondairy butter

Preparation

1. In a baking pan, add together the diced apples and frozen berries.

2. Next combine the flour, cinnamon, sugar and butter in a small bowl and then spoon over the fruit. Sprinkle a little flour over all so that there are no exposed parts of the fruit.

3. Transfer to basket, if you want. Place the pressure cooker trivet in the inner steel pot. Place the pan/ basket on the trivet. Place the Crisp Lid on top of the inner pot and plug it in.

4. Set to 350°F and cook for 20 minutes

Per Serving: Calories 310; Total Fat 12g; Protein 2g; Total Carb 50g; Sodium: Cholesterol: 31mg; Fiber: 5g

Moist Coffee Choco Cake

Prep Time: 10 minutes

Cook Time: 10 minutes

Servings: 4

Ingredients

1 cup of vegan dark chocolate, chopped

½ cup of brown sugar

½ cup of vegan butter

1/3 cup flour

2 tablespoons of aquafaba

Juice of ½ of an orange

½ teaspoon of instant coffee

½ teaspoon of baking powder

Salt

Preparation

1. Melt the butter and chocolate. Once fully melted, add the orange juice and mix well.

2. Add together the aquafaba, sugar and the coffee in a bowl. Beat with an electric mixer to make creamy. Add the chocolate mix and mix thoroughly to combine.

3. Add the baking powder, the flour and salt and then stir.

4. Transfer dough to a greased baking pan and place on the trivet in the pot. Plug Crisp Lid.

5. Set to 400°F and cook 10 minutes.

Per Serving: Calories 591; Total Fat 46g; Protein 2g; Total Carb 45g; Sodium:282mg; Cholesterol: 61mg: Fiber: 1g

Fried Doughnuts

Prep Time: 15 minutes

Cook Time: 10minutes

Servings: 9 yields

Ingredients

1 tablespoon cold nondairy butter

1/4 cup plus 1 tablespoon coconut sugar, divided

½ tablespoon vegan egg yolk of choice

1 tablespoons water

1 cup + 1 tablespoon all-purpose flour, unbleached

¾ teaspoons baking powder

½ teaspoon salt

1/4 cup plain nondairy yogurt

Cooking spray

1 teaspoon ground cinnamon

Preparation

1. Add together in bowl; the butter and ¼ cup sugar, mixing well.

2. Whisk egg replacer and water in a smaller bowl and add it to the mixed butter and sugar.

3. Combine the flour, baking powder and the salt in a medium bowl and add to the butter mixture. Mix and then add the yoghurt, folding in to form a dough.

4. Roll into 9 balls, place on parchment paper. Spray fryer basket with cooking spray and place balls in the fryer basket. Place the pressure cooker trivet in the inner steel pot. Place the basket on the trivet. Place the Crisp Lid on top of the inner pot and plug it in.

5. Set to 360°F and cook 10 minutes, flipping halfway through.

6. Combine on a plate; the 1 tablespoon of sugar that's left and cinnamon. Roll the cooked doughnut balls in the cinnamon sugar and place to cool on a rack.

Per Serving: Calories 105; Total Fat 1g; Protein 2g; Total Carb 9g; Sodium:193mg; Cholesterol: 0mg: Fiber: 2g

Crunchy Cookies

Prep Time: 12 minutes

Cook Time: 10minutes

Servings: 6

Ingredients

8 ½ oz. of chilled vegan chocolate chip cookie dough

¼ cup of crumbs, graham cracker

1 tablespoons of sugar

2 tablespoons melted vegan butter

Preparation

1. Make 6 ball pieces of the cookie dough.

2. Next, add together the sugar and crumbs in a bowl.

3. Coat the dough in the butter and then dip in the crumb mixture. Place all the coated balls on a baking pan and put the pan in the freezer to freeze for 3 hours, or overnight, if possible.

3. Line the fryer basket with aluminum foil and place the balls on it, ensuring that they are well- spread out. Place on trivet and Plud in Crisp Lid.

4. Set to cook for 350°F at 10 minutes. Enjoy with a glass of milk.

Spiced Apples
Gluten-free, dairy-free and delicious!

Prep Time: 5 minutes

Cook Time: 15minutes

Servings: 4

Ingredients

4 small apples, sliced

2 tablespoons coconut oil

1 teaspoon apple pie spice

2 tablespoons sugar

Preparation

1. Place apples in a bowl, drizzle coconut oil, sprinkle with apple pie spice and with sugar and then stir to coat the apples evenly.

2. Transfer apples to a small pan and place on trivet. Plug in Crisp Lid. Set to 350°F for 15 minutes.

3. Remove the tender apples and enjoy with ice cream.

Per Serving: Calories 165; Total Fat 7g; Protein 0g; Total Carb 28g; Sodium:0mg; Cholesterol: 0mg; Fiber: 5g

Marshmallow Chocolate Bread Pudding

Prep Time: 15 minutes

Cook Time: 30 minutes

Servings: 2

Ingredients

4 croissants, cut into 1 inch cubes

2 cups of coconut cream

½ cup of mini marshmallows

¼ cup of vegan chocolate chips

¾ cup of sugar

2 tablespoons of aquafaba

1 teaspoon of pure vanilla extract

1 teaspoon of fresh lemon juice

Pinch kosher salt

Preparation

1. Add together the coconut cream, aquafaba, the lemon juice the, sugar and the vanilla in a blender and blend to smoothness.

2. Place the croissant in the fryer basket, set in on trivet in the pot and toast at a temperature of 400°F for 5 minutes. Remove and place in the coconut cream mixture to soak.

3. Spray pan with cooking spray. Add the chocolate chips and the marshmallows to the cream mixture, mix well and add to the pan.

4. Place on trivet and plug in Crisp Lid. Cook at 340°F for 25 minutes.

Crispy Caramelized Bananas

The Airfryer makes bananas that are crispy inside and caramelized and when you taste it, they are so soft and delish! Enjoy as is or top as desired!

Prep Time: 1 minutes

Cook Time: 8 minutes

Servings: 1

Ingredients

2 bananas

1 1/2 teaspoon of lemon juice

1 tablespoon of coconut sugar

Preparation

1. Do not peel; but wash the bananas and then slice lengthwise, straight down. Drizzle with lemon juice and sprinkle with coconut sugar.

2. Line the fryer basket with parchment paper and place the bananas on it. Place the pressure cooker trivet in the inner steel pot. Place the basket on the trivet. Place the Crisp Lid on top of the inner pot and plug it in.

3. Cook at 400°F for 8 minutes.

4. Enjoy alone or top with nuts, cinnamon or coconut cream.

Per Serving: Calories 390; Total Fat 2g; Protein 8g; Total Carb 108g; Sodium:8mg; Cholesterol: 0mg; Fiber: 5g

Banana S'mores

Another addictive version of a banana dessert!

Prep Time: 10 minutes

Cook Time: 8 minutes

Servings: 4

Ingredients

4 unpeeled bananas

3 tablespoons of mini semi-sweet vegan chocolate chips

3 tablespoons of mini vegan marshmallows

3 tablespoons of graham cracker cereal

3 tablespoons of mini peanut butter chips

Preparation

1. Cut the bananas lengthwise but do not cut through to the bottom. Open the banana slightly to make a pocket.

2. In each of the pocket, fill with the marshmallows, chocolate chips and the peanut butter chips. Add the graham cracker as well, pushing inside. .

3. Place the filed bananas in the fryer basket, Place the pressure cooker trivet in the inner steel pot. Place the basket on the trivet. Place the Crisp Lid on top of the inner pot and plug it in.

4. Cook at 400°F for 8 minutes. Dessert is ready once the marshmallows and the chocolate is melted, the banana is softened, and its peel are black in color.

5. Let it rest for about 5 minutes. Serve afterwards.

Per Serving: Calories 230; Total Fat 6g; Protein 2g; Total Carb 46g; Sodium:46mg; Cholesterol: 0mg: Fiber: 4g

Pumpkin Spice Baked Apples

To bring out the best in this recipe, core the apples without slicing them completely through the bottom. Place your knife at a slight angle when piercing the apple, remove the top, scoop the rest out with a spoon, top up with the pumpkin spice filling and place in your Crisp Lid. Viola!

Prep Time: 10 minutes

Cook Time: 25 minutes

Servings: 4

Ingredients

4 apples, cored

1/4 cup maple syrup

1/3 cup rolled oats

1/4 cup pecans, chopped

2 tablespoons raisins

1 teaspoon pumpkin spice seasoning

2/3 cup water

Preparation

1. Core the apples. Combine the rest of the ingredients, but not the water, in a bowl.

2. Pour the water into a round baking pan/dish. Transfer the apples to the pan. Place the pressure cooker trivet in the inner steel pot. Place the pan on the trivet. Place the Crisp Lid on top of the inner pot and plug it in.

3. Cook at 350°F for 15 minutes. Do not shake. Remove once apples are tender once pierced with a fork. Otherwise, cook for 2 to 3 more minutes.

Per Serving: Calories 211; Total Fat 5g; Protein 7g; Total Carb 55g; Sodium: 6mg; Cholesterol: 0mg: Fiber: 2g

Chocolate Mug Cake
An irresistible treat!

Prep Time: 2 minutes

Cook Time: 10 minutes

Servings: 1

Ingredients:

¼ cup of flour

5 tablespoons of sugar

3 teaspoons of coconut oil

3 tablespoons of coconut milk

1 tablespoon of cocoa powder

Preparation

1. Combine all the ingredients in a mug and place in the fryer basket.

2. Place the pressure cooker trivet in the inner steel pot. Place the basket on the trivet. Place the Crisp Lid on top of the inner pot and plug it in.

3. Set at 392°F and cook for 10 minutes.

Per Serving: Calories 503; Total Fat 15g; Protein 4g; Total Carb 91g; Sodium: 15mg; Cholesterol: 0mg: Fiber: 3g

Concluded

Printed in Great Britain
by Amazon